# HAMSTERS

Hamlyn
## PET CARE
Handbooks

# HAMSTERS

**Joyce and Keith
Lawrence**

**HAMLYN**

Published by
The Hamlyn Publishing Group Limited
Bridge House, 69 London Road
Twickenham, Middlesex TW1 3SB, England
and distributed for them by
Octopus Distribution Services Limited
Rushden, Northamptonshire NN10 9RZ, England

First published 1987

ISBN 0 600 55141 5

Some of the material in this book
is reproduced from other books published
by The Hamlyn Publishing Group Ltd.

Printed in Hong Kong by Mandarin Offset

# Contents

# Introduction

The golden hamster was first described by an English explorer named Waterhouse, returning from an expedition in the Syrian Desert in 1839. He not only gave a precise description but also brought back the skin of a specimen. There the story seemed to have ended, and by the beginning of this century it was thought that the golden hamster was extinct.

But it was not extinct: exactly 91 years later, in 1930, a zoologist named Professor Aharoni found a single female golden hamster with a litter of 12 young, when he excavated a burrow more than 2 m (7 ft) deep at a site near Aleppo in Syria.

Since that time there have been hardly any records of anyone finding golden hamsters again in the wild, and it seems that all today's pet golden hamsters are descended from this single family captured in Syria. Indeed, only three of Aharoni's specimens survived in captivity, but the professor found his hamsters to be prolific breeders. In the first year he raised more than 150 hamsters!

The golden hamster was first introduced into the UK in 1931, and some individuals were exported to America in 1938. It was not until after 1945 that the hamster's potential as a disease-free and amenable pet was recognized. It is now one of the most popular small pets, and many colour varieties have been developed. There are numerous clubs and societies, and shows and exhibitions for these animals are commonplace.

While golden hamsters are now available in a range of colour varieties, the original-coloured form is still by far the most popular variety. The natural colouring of the golden hamster is a rich golden brown with a white belly, the face being marked with white patches beneath almost black cheek flashes.

An average adult golden hamster is about 15 cm (6 in) in length, measured from the nose to the tip of the rather stumpy tail. The fur is thick and glossy and the skin is rather loose. It may seem strange for a desert-living animal such as a hamster to have a thick coat, but it must be remembered that the hamster is not active above ground during the heat of the day. It comes out only during the extreme cold of the desert night. The paws are good at grasping and the hamster uses them both to grasp branches and food, and to groom itself.

Like all rodents, the hamster must constantly gnaw to prevent its incisor teeth from growing too long. The animal's eyesight is rather poor, but its hearing is acute. This is hardly surprising as in the wild the hamster would spend the day in its darkened burrows, coming out only at night. Therefore it has evolved a reliance on its hearing to avoid predators.

One of the distinguishing features of the hamster is its cheek pouches. This is an extremely important adaptation for a desert-living rodent, as it enables the animal to scour large areas of the countryside for food, stuffing whatever it finds into its cheek pouches. When they are stuffed full,

*A Golden Hamster with her young;* **below:** *in the wild hamsters live in a series of burrows*

the hamster can transport the food back to its hoard in the burrow. It is from this habit of hoarding food that the animal gets its name: *Hamster* is German for a hoarder.

A golden hamster is an excellent family pet, and to many its solitary nature is an added advantage, for companion animals are not necessary. Golden hamsters should always be housed singly, from five weeks of age, to prevent fighting. This fighting will inevitably lead to the death of one of the animals, and indeed the only time golden hamsters should be brought together is very briefly for mating.

Hamsters are not recommended as pets for children under eight years old, who are likely to have difficulties in handling them, and in consequence could be bitten.

Hamsters are said to be nocturnal in their habits and this is certainly true of the golden hamster, but not of the other hamster species such as the common (European) hamster or the Chinese hamster. These two species are 'crepuscular' which means that they are active at dawn and dusk. Being active in the evening, golden hamsters are suitable pets for people who are absent from the house during most of the day. The animal enjoys exercise and will scamper around the cage playing with toys, making and remaking its bed, storing food, gnawing, grooming and attempting to escape.

Golden hamsters are very easy to keep and are extremely clean animals if cared for properly. They are undemanding in their accommodation requirements, and can be housed in a much more confined space than many other small pets. However, they do have one disadvantage: the hamster's lifespan is relatively short, about 18–24 months, and many live for less than one year. Cases have been recorded of hamsters living for seven years (and one even for ten years) but these are unusual.

Strange as it may seem, there are reports of escaped golden hamsters breeding successfully as wild populations in Britain. They have proved to be rather a pest because of their prolific breeding and their gnawing habits. To illustrate how quickly they can breed in the British climate, in the autumn of 1957 six golden hamsters escaped from a pet shop in Bath. One year later 50 were caught in the shop's basement. It is now illegal in the UK to release hamsters into the wild deliberately.

# Choosing
# and buying

Unlike the rabbit, there are few shapes and sizes of hamster to choose from, although there are many colour varieties of the golden hamster. The golden hamster (sometimes known as the Syrian hamster) is a species of animal known to science as *Mesocricetus auratus*.

Three other species of hamster are kept as pets: the Chinese hamster (*Cricetelus griseus*), the Russian hamster (*Phodopus sungorus*) and Common or European hamster (*Cricetus cricetus*), which is also called the black-bellied hamster.

Golden hamsters should preferably be bought from pet shops or accredited suppliers where only good quality breeding stock is maintained. Hamsters are among the few animals which should not be bought from the amateur breeder without careful investigation, as the line may be weakened from too much inbreeding. Some experts are worried that hamsters may possibly carry infections that can spread to man and cause serious illness, but supplies from accredited sources are screened to eliminate this risk.

All hamsters have a tendency to bite, especially if they are not handled correctly or are untamed. Because of this you should purchase youngsters of approximately six to eight weeks of age so that they can be readily finger-tamed. Golden hamsters unfortunately tend to fight to the death if kept together, so that even breeding pairs can be housed together only briefly, at mating.

It makes little difference whether you purchase a male or a female, as the lifespan and temperament are basically the same.

## Golden hamster checklist

When purchasing a golden hamster a number of points should be checked and you should examine the animal carefully, using the following list as a guide:

## HAMSTERS

**1** Daytime drowsiness is of course normal as the hamster is a nocturnal animal.

**2** Be careful when disturbing sleeping hamsters if you want a closer look – they will bite if frightened.

**3** If the hamster is awake it should be very active, being quick, alert and intensely interested in its environment.

**4** The faeces should be confined to one area of the cage – the hamster's 'toilet' – and should be solid, well formed and dark brown in colour.

**Nose** The nose is pink, moist and clean, and should have no discharge. If the hamster is awake the nose is constantly twitching.

**Eyes** Clear and bright, no discharge. Eye colour may be black, ruby or red according to colour variety, and albino hamsters have pink eyes.

**Ears** Erect and free from scabs, torn edges and waxy discharge. Young golden hamsters should always have hairy ears, which become balder as the animal ages.

**Teeth** The teeth show yellowish discoloration and they should be growing parallel and not overlong. The upper teeth should be outside the lower teeth when the mouth is closed.

*Erect ears, clear bright eyes, a clean damp nose and an alert air are signs of a healthy hamster*

**Mouth** Clean; check for a foul smell from the mouth, which may be associated with a pouch infection, as would drooling and dribbling.

**Coat** Glossy and well groomed, with no obvious areas of hair loss, sores or wounds. Ensure that the coat is not tangled or matted in the long-haired varieties. Examine under the tail to see that it is dry and clean. Any wetness in this area may be the first signs of a condition known as 'wet tail' (see Ailments section).

**Feet** There should be no missing or damaged claws, and they should be short and well-trimmed.

## The common hamster

This animal (also known as the European hamster or the black-bellied hamster) is very different from the golden hamster, being nearly five times the size. It grows up to 30 cm (12 in) in length and weighs up to 500 g (1 lb). It is dark grey with rufous guard hairs and it has chestnut cheek and eye patches. The flanks, ears and nose are white.

The common hamster ranges widely throughout most of Europe. In some parts of the continent it is so numerous that it is an agricultural pest, eating grain from farmers' fields and granaries. A single common hamster will collect up to 50 kg (100 lb) of food in its winter store.

In the past farmers in areas plagued by these hamsters

used to dig up the animals' grain hoards for use as cattle feed. In some countries a 'bounty' was offered for their dead bodies. Indeed, in the early 18th century hamsters used to be hunted as game in Prussia and Saxony, although recipes on how to cook them have not survived.

The common hamster has a gestation period of about three weeks and in the wild it produces two litters per year of four to eight young. Three weeks after birth the young are weaned and leave the burrow to lead an independent life. In view of its size and aggressive behaviour, the common hamster is not the most suitable family pet.

## The Chinese hamster

This species has gained in popularity during the 1980s, possibly because it is easier to handle than the golden hamster and less aggressive to its own kind. It has been described as the 'sociable' hamster. It is one of the smaller species of hamster, reaching at most 10 cm (4 in) in length (nose to tail tip) and weighing 50 g ($1\frac{1}{2}$ oz) when adult.

The Chinese hamster is browny grey in colour with a much darker stripe down the centre of the back, and an off-white belly. A single colour mutation has been described, the Spotted variety. While Chinese hamsters may seem quarrelsome among themselves this type of behaviour is totally different from the overt agrression exhibited by the golden hamster; they are social animals and should be kept in groups.

The most useful form of housing is an aquarium with an escape-proof lid. This is because it is all too easy for young Chinese hamsters to squeeze through the bars of a normal hamster cage. The gestation period is about three weeks and litters of eight to ten young are not uncommon; however, many females will reduce the litter to six or even four by killing the weaker cubs. The average lifespan is about two years.

## The Russian hamster

This species has been offered to the pet trade in recent years. It has many of the features of the Chinese hamster but is said to be less quarrelsome, having an impeccable family life.

# Varieties of golden hamster

During 56 years in captivity, golden hamsters have multiplied into the millions, and breeders have developed many differently coloured varieties which are all the same in body size and shape. The colour that is by far the most common in pet shops and in homes is the original or 'natural' colour of the animal, as it was when it lived in the wild. In this book, we shall spell this 'natural' variety with capital letters: Golden Hamster. Without capitals, the name golden hamster refers to all varieties of the animal, for example, when giving details of feeding or general care, which apply to them all.

## Golden Hamster

The variety subdivides into three, according to fur shade; all have black eyes:

**Normal Golden** The coat is basically golden with dark tips to the hairs and greyish roots. The abdomen is white and the animal has dark grey ears.

**Dark Golden** There is a reddish sheen to the coat and the black tips to the hairs are much more pronounced. The ears are black.

**Light Golden** The black tips to the hairs are absent. The abdomen is white.

## Cream Hamsters

Unlike the Golden Hamster, the coat colour is constant but the eyes are different. There are three different eye colours in this variety: Red-eyed Cream, Ruby-eyed Cream and Black-eyed Cream. The last was one of the earliest colours to be bred. This variety also has a deeper tone of coat than the other two varieties, as well as darker ears.

*The Golden Hamster is also known as the Syrian hamster because the ancestor of all pet Golden Hamsters was found in Syria*

*The Dark Grey and Ruby-eyed Cream are two of the many colour variations which have been bred*

# Grey Hamsters

Again there are three shades of Grey Hamster. They are all fairly new varieties.

**Dominant Grey** This variety has black eyes and ears. The coat is dark grey overlaid with a flesh coloured tint.

**Dark Grey** This is dark grey overall with black ears and eyes.

**Light Grey** The distinctive red eyes in this variety make it easily recognizable. It has a silvery tinge to the coat.

# White and Albino Hamsters

There are two varieties of Albino Hamster as well as a White Hamster.

**Albino** This is completely white with pink eyes.

**Dark-eared Albino** As the name suggests, this is nearly an Albino but has dark ears.

**Black-eyed White** The coat is white, the ears are pink and the eyes black.

## Other colours

**Cinnamon** This is the brightest coloured hamster, with a rich orange fur and lighter ears.

**Yellow** This is similar to the Black-eyed Cream but the fur is slightly darker with darker guard hairs, which the Cream does not have.

**Honey** This variety resembles the Yellow, but has red eyes and lighter ears.

**Rust** The fur is darker than that of the Cinnamon; ears are brown and eyes are black.

**Left to right:** *Black-eyed White, Golden, Cinnamon, Grey, and Fawn colour varieties of baby hamster*

*A Cinnamon-and-white and an Albino Long-haired hamster*

**Sepia** Although sometimes confused with the Grey Hamster, this is in fact more beige than grey. The eyes are black and the ears grey.

**Smoke Pearl** The coat is completely pearl grey, the eyes are black and the ears are dark grey.

**Blond** The fur is blond and the eyes are red.

**Dove** The fur is medium grey with dark bases; the abdomen is white. The eyes are black with dark grey ears.

## Marked colours

**Banded** These hamsters have an unbroken band of white circling the body. The fur can be any colour, and examples include the Light-grey Banded, Cinna-

*A White Band golden hamster*

mon Banded, Cream Banded, Golden Banded, Honey Banded, Ruby-eyed Fawn Banded and Tortoiseshell Banded.

**Piebald** The Piebald Hamster is basically white with patches of colour rather like the piebald horse. Piebald Hamsters tend to be smaller than normal and the females do not make good mothers.

**Dominant Spot** This variety has begun to replace the Piebald Hamster as the markings are very similar, but the hamsters are not undersized and the females make good mothers.

**Mosaic** One or more dark coloured markings on a pale coat.

**Tortoiseshell and White** These hamsters are very similar in pattern to the tortoiseshell cat. The coat is overlaid with golden and white patches. There is a banded variety of this hamster. There are also Cinnamon Tortoiseshells and Grey Tortoiseshells but the colour contrast is less than in the white.

## Rare colour varieties

Some colours have remained rare, especially the Ruby-eyed Fawn and the Ruby-eyed Cream. This is because most males of these colour varieties are infertile, or are fertile for only a short period of time after reaching maturity. Even if a successful mating takes place, the females are such bad mothers that few young are raised to maturity.

*A Tortoiseshell and White and a Cinnamon hamster*

## Coat varieties

Most hamsters are shorthaired varieties, but there are three other main fur types, which are available in any of the colours described above.

**Satin** This is very similar to the shorthaired but the coat has a glossy sheen which makes the colours look much richer.

*A satinised long-haired hamster*

*A long-haired hamster*

**Longhaired** The coat is long, fine and dense. This type of coat needs to be groomed regularly as it tends to become tangled. The longest coat is found in the males but it does not reach its maximum length until they are at least six months old.

**Rex** The coat of the Rex is in a class of its own, being long, dense and curly. The young hamsters have a wavy coat. The whiskers are also curled.

# Housing

## Cages

Hamsters are rodents and need to gnaw constantly to wear down their large incisor teeth to prevent them becoming overgrown. Any housing bought for a hamster must therefore be able to withstand constant attack by their front teeth. An appropriate size of cage for a single male or a female and her litter is at least 60 × 30 × 20 cm (24 × 12 × 8 in).

You can build a wooden cage yourself, using hard woods or Formica covered plywood, ensuring that all exposed edges are metal bound to limit the damage caused by gnawing. Seal the joints with resin for a watertight fit. Fit a glass or mesh front, either as a sliding

**Right:** *minimum requirements for a hamster cage are a nesting box and exercise equipment;* **below:** *different levels in a cage provide exercise and play possibilities*

door or as a pull-down flap. The main benefit of making your own cage is that imagination is the only limit to the complexity of the design.

Commercially available cages are usually made from plastic, although all-metal designs are still available. The plastic cages have a tray surmounted by a metal barred framework, with access through a spring-loaded door in the top. Many varieties are available, but they should have a floor area of at least 1,250 sq cm (200 sq in).

One of the most satisfactory of these cages is the Rotastak range. This is an elaborate system of inter-connected, ventilated, round plastic modules which imitate a natural burrow system. This system is infinitely

*More elaborate hamster housing partly recreates the series of burrows which the animals inhabit in the wild*

*An entertaining attraction in its own right, this space station type hamster housing is well adapted to the creature's needs*

expandable, with a variety of modules available. However, the system does have some minor faults. The tubes connecting different levels are vertical, totally unlike the natural burrow which would normally slope at some 60° to the horizontal. This restricts the movement of young animals.

Although expensive and suffering from some minor disadvantages, the Rotastak system does allow for easy cleaning, and it is long-lasting and easily assembled. Handling of the hamsters in the system is very easy, and individuals can be readily isolated in a single unit. All exposed edges of the interconnecting tubes must be protected by anti-gnawing rings – if not, the tubes will rapidly shorten.

Hamster cages are also available in the shape of bird cages. An all-glass aquarium with a well-fitting wire top can make an ideal home for a hamster. Choose a tank at least 45 cm (18 in) long with a floor area of approximately 1,250 sq cm (200 sq in).

## Accessories

**Exercise wheels and playballs** The most commonly purchased accessory, and certainly the most appreciated by the hamster, is an exercise wheel. A number of different types are available, but unfortunately many designs are positively dangerous and should be avoided. Do not buy a metal wheel with open spokes and an open framework for the hamster to run on. Even though this wheel will last well, being gnaw-proof, it often causes leg fractures if the hamster slips. Wheels with plastic spokes are less dangerous but are often destroyed within days, victims of the hamster's teeth.

*Exercise wheels are popular and much used accessories for active hamsters*

The only wheels that can be recommended are those that have a solid back and floor with an open front. There are no spokes, nor has the treadmill an open-frame through which the hamsters' legs can slip.

A recent development of the exercise wheel is the playball. This is a clear plastic sphere into which the hamster is placed. The ball can then be propelled freely around the floor or mounted on a metal frame. It must be admitted, however, that playballs are open to abuse, and because of this they should only be used under the direct supervision of a responsible adult. Properly used, the playball will provide a hamster with hours of pleasure. To ensure that the playballs are not abused a number of recommendations are set out below:

**1** The hamster must become accustomed to the ball by being placed in it for no more than a few minutes initially. This time can be gradually increased to a maximum of 20 minutes twice daily.

*Hamsters need an enclosed nesting box for breeding and other hamsters can enjoy hiding away in such a box*

**2** Playballs should not be used in direct sunlight. Even though they are ventilated, the temperature inside may rise very quickly, for the plastic acts just like a greenhouse.

**3** Never allow the use of a playball near the top of a flight of stairs or on a table top, unless on its stand. A fall from such a height would probably kill the enclosed hamster.

**4** Place only one hamster in the ball at a time and wash the ball in clean, warm water between animals.

**5** Ensure that there are no cats or dogs in the room; they may chase the ball and frighten the hamster.

Used as suggested, playballs are the safest of the exercise wheels, being the least likely to cause injury. They are unlikely to be gnawed as no edges are exposed, but even if they were they are made of non-toxic materials.

**Nest box** Any hamster will find a nest box useful as a convenient extra hiding place, but if you breed your hamsters you will have to install one of these. It is simply a wooden box, with metal lining covering any gnawable

*The real thing would soon be gnawed to shreds, but an earthenware replica of a boot makes an amusing addition to a hamster cage*

edges, a minimum of 15 cm (6 in) square. The entrance hole should be just big enough for a pregnant female to get in. If your hamster lives in a metal cage, fix the box high up above floor level. For an all-metal cage, where the nest box is normally placed at a height above floor level, you will need to place suitably sized ladders and branches for the hamster to climb up into the box.

**Other accessories** Gnaw-proof earthenware ornaments in the form of an old boot full of holes or a holed barrel can be bought from your local petshop.

You should also provide wooden objects and twigs for the hamster to chew on, such as pieces of soft wood and branches of apple, blackthorn, hawthorn or willow, as well as a few nuts.

The safest way of all to provide chewing opportunities is to use specially prepared 'wood gnaws'. These are blocks of *Ochroma lagapus* wood which is non-toxic and hard enough to ensure adequate tooth wear. They come in a variety of shapes and sizes and are free of wood stains, varnish and pesticides.

*A variety of playthings which it can explore, move and gnaw will help expend your pet's boundless energy*

# Handling

Confidence is essential when handling hamsters, but this only comes with practice and you must expect an occasional nip before you gain your hamster's trust.

Newly purchased hamsters often prove difficult to handle, and this is especially true of those bred by the major accredited breeders. This is because the hamsters are rarely handled prior to dispatch to the pet shops. This can be particularly disappointing to children when their newly acquired pet will try to escape and attempt to bite.

When handling a hamster for the first time, allow it to smell your hands before attempting to pick it up. For the first few days after purchase, do nothing more than use this opportunity to offer titbits and to stroke the animal. Too early an attempt at picking up may cause the hamster

*Pick up your hamster gently from beneath*

*Carry your pet with your hands cupped around, but be careful not to squeeze it*

to jump unexpectedly, which could lead to injury to the hamster; or it may bite you.

# How to pick up a hamster

The first attempts at handling should be limited to gently scooping it up and allowing it to sit in your cupped hands just above the floor of the cage, so that if it does make an attempt to escape it does not have far to fall. When the hamster has become used to being handled in this way, you can use either of two methods to lift it: (1) place the palm of your hand over the body, with the hamster's head facing towards the wrist, then curl your fingers around the hamster's abdomen; or (2) lift it by the loose skin at the back of the neck with the thumb and first finger, while supporting the body weight with your free hand. Hold the hamster firmly but do not squeeze it as this will cause it to react violently. Never disturb a sleeping hamster, as it will certainly resent this and bite.

Hamsters are very nervous and easily frightened when young, so cage cleaning and initial handling should be done very quietly and as gently as possible, with no sudden movements. It is often a good idea to whisper to them during handling, to avoid startling them.

*Pick up hamsters in this way only once they are completely used to being handled*

## Children and hamsters

Children under eight years old should not be encouraged to handle hamsters unless supervised by a competent adult. Inept handling by the child will lead to a bite, and once a hamster has a grip on a finger it is usually very reluctant to let go. Such a bad experience could colour a young child's attitude to pets for the rest of his or her life.

Because a hamster may make unexpected attempts at escape, all children should be encouraged either to sit on the floor while playing with a hamster or to sit at a table. A hamster dropped from even a child's height is usually a dead hamster.

# General care

## Floor litter

Flooring of the cage should not only provide the hamster with material for shredding to make bedding, but must also be absorbent. Cover the floor of the cage with at least five or six sheets of newspaper, topped with 2.5 cm (1 in) of sawdust and/or woodshavings. Toilet tissue, kitchen towels, hay and cardboard can also be added. You can then leave the hamster to shred and arrange the materials as it feels fit. Peat, cat litter and zeolite (a natural resin) have also been suggested as flooring materials and may prove particularly useful in the area of the hamster's 'toilet'.

## Nest box litter

Many of the materials recommended for this purpose have proved troublesome, especially long-stranded, man-made synthetic materials and natural fibres such as wool. These products have killed hamsters because they are indigestible: the animals swallow the long fibres and these block the intestine. There have also been reports of limbs becoming entwined in long strands of fibre which act like a tourniquet, with subsequent loss of or injury to the affected limb.

The only nesting materials that can be recommended are shredded, paper-based beddings and the recently introduced artificial fur bedding. Many people still prefer to provide more natural nesting materials such as soft hay, but this should be short-chopped and dust-free. In very hot weather hamsters may move their nests out of the nest box; however, the nest box should be left in the cage as the hamsters will return the nest to its original place as soon as the weather cools.

## Hamster toilet

Hamsters are very clean animals and usually select a specific area of their cage in which to urinate. Unless this area is cleaned regularly it will rapidly start to produce a strong smell. If you provide a specially designed 'toilet'

*This long-haired hamster has something to gnaw, somewhere to burrow and somewhere to explore, all favourite hamster activities*

area, as far as possible from the sleeping or nesting quarters, they will almost certainly use it. This area can be designed to make daily cleaning relatively easy. Take a shallow tray, such as the polystyrene food trays used in supermarkets, and fill it with cat litter or sawdust. Top this with a small amount of soiled litter and it will encourage

the hamster to use this as its toilet. It is then only a few moments' work to change this tray daily.

## Housekeeping

**Cleaning** Clean out the hamster's toilet area daily, and clean out the cage completely once each week. Remove the bedding but retain a small portion. Wash the cage thoroughly with warm, soapy water, rinse it and allow it to dry. Take out all the floor litter and replace it with clean material. When you put in new bedding, mix in the portion of old bedding that you have kept, so that the hamster returns to a cage with a familiar smell.

**Airing** Hamsters should be kept indoors except during the hottest summer days, when you can place the cage outside but in the shade. You should ensure that the cage remains in the shade as the day progresses. The major problem, however, associated with putting hamsters outdoors is that they will certainly attract the attention of all the local cats. This is unlikely to be a pleasant experience for the hamsters.

**Temperature** It is particularly important during the winter to ensure an equitable temperature at night because hamsters can become dormant and even appear dead if the temperature falls below 4°C (40°F). The problem arises because central heating systems are normally switched off during the night and room temperatures can plummet by the early morning. So if you find an apparently dead hamster one morning, place it somewhere warm such as the airing cupboard before you attempt to bury it. This has resurrected many 'dead' hamsters. To prevent it happening again, you may need to fit a small local source of heat such as a light bulb or an undercage heating pad.

# Food containers

Hamster food can be bought boxed or loose. Whichever way it is bought, buy only the minimum quantity possible, and store it in airtight plastic food containers. This will ensure that the food remains as fresh as possible and does not become stale. The food containers should not be kept in the kitchen or in the general vicinity of human food or food preparation areas. Always wash your hands after handling hamster food or their food bowls. The plastic containers should not be washed along with crockery or utensils used by the family.

# Exercise

Hamsters enjoy leaving their cage for exercise, and while the table top may be an ideal playground, they must be closely supervised to prevent any injuries caused by falls. Playing with the hamster on the floor will of course

*An enclosed playball can be a slightly safer variation on the exercise wheel*

eliminate injuries from falls, but it may lead to its disappearance into the skirting board or under the floorboards. Hamsters are expert escapologists.

No matter how careful you are in trying to prevent your hamster escaping, it will happen one day. Attempts to recapture the animal tend to turn into a mini rodeo, with the animal being poked, prodded and frightened in an attempt to drive it towards its would-be captor. Many capture attempts lead to the death of the hamster from fright and exhaustion, or the complete loss of the hamster as it escapes from the house.

**How to catch a hamster** Two methods have been proposed for recapture, the 'scoop' and the 'pitfall trap'. The scoop is simply an open tin, box or cardboard tube which is presented to the animal as a bolthole. If slowly positioned in front of the hamster it is surprising how often it will run straight in. A hand placed over the open end completes the trap.

The other method, the 'pitfall trap' requires a 5 litre (2 gallon) ice cream container or a plastic bucket. The hamster is provided with a ramp or stairway so that it can have easy access to the food which is placed in the bottom of the container. Once the hamser has climbed into the container it will be unable to scale the smooth vertical walls, and there it will sit until you return it to its cage.

*A hamster which has escaped can be tempted by an intriguing ramp leading to some food in an escape-proof container*

# Feeding

## Hoarding

Hamster comes from the German word meaning 'hoarder' and collecting food and gathering it into a food store is characteristic of this group of rodents. They will rarely eat all the food you provide at one go but will store part of the meal and return to this hoard at intervals during the day.

To carry this food around, hamsters have developed two large cheek pouches which can be packed with food. The cheek pouches are quite separate from the rest of the

*Hamsters' cheek pouches can hold a surprising amount of food for future eating*

mouth and are entered via a gap between the front and cheek teeth. This gap is termed the 'diastema'. The pouches are emptied into the food stores which will be located in a number of places in the cage, including the sleeping quarters.

The habit of storing food can give rise to problems as some types of food such as fruit and titbits, cheese and earthworms, can start to decay. Souring of the stored food leads to foul smells in the cage and digestive upsets if eaten by the hamster. While hamsters can resent their food stores being raided, it is essential to remove soured food regularly. The habit of hoarding, however, can be used to your advantage if you are going away for the weekend, for the hamster will draw upon its stored food when it becomes hungry.

# Diet

An adult hamster should be provided with about 15 g ($\frac{1}{2}$ oz) of food once a day, preferably in the evening when it is becoming active. In the wild the hamster's diet would be based on seeds, with access to plant material after the seasonal rains. Small grubs, insects and possibly carrion, make up the remainder of the wild hamster's diet.

**Grains, seeds and nuts** In captivity your hamster will need a balanced diet of assorted grains and nuts, and you can buy this at any pet shop. The most convenient way to purchase this type of diet is in packets, but buy only the smallest amount available, to ensure the food is always fresh.

Alternatively you can make up your own mixture, using assorted grains including flaked and whole maize, assorted bird seeds, including millet and hemp, broken dog biscuits and rabbit pellets.

While hamsters are particularly fond of sunflower seeds, these should be provided only in small quantities because of their high oil content. Too many sunflower seeds will lead to a little, tubby, overweight pet which will die before its time.

You may like to offer toasted stale bread and cake, crusts and biscuits, in small quantities. These all have the benefit that the hamster can store them for some time before they begin to deteriorate.

*Hamsters enjoy holding and gnawing their food; large and solid items are no problem to them*

**Greens and fruit** If offered, hamsters will eat relatively large amounts of greens and fruit. Cabbage, kale, lettuce, watercress and other salad greenstuffs will be eaten with relish, as will slices of fruit such as apple and pear. Carrots, swede and turnip are a useful source of food during the winter, when greens are scarce and expensive. Tinned or frozen vegetables can also be used to augment winter diets.

Hamsters will take raisins, currants and sultanas, but you should reserve these as special treats.

If a hamster has access to a lot of fruit and vegetables it will usually drink only small amounts of water. This is normal because of the high water content of this type of food.

**Wild plants** Certain species of wild plants offer a free source of food for your pet, especially during the spring and summer. Such plants include chickweed, clover,

*Hamsters need green food in their diet and clover (left) and dandelion (right) are both suitable*

*Mealworms, cheese and toast provide protein but should be given only occasionally*

coltsfoot, cow parsley, dandelion, docks, groundsel, plantain, sorrel, vetches and fresh grass. All green foods should be well washed and shaken dry before use, and only small quantities should be offered at a time.

Many plants are poisonous and should be avoided. These include bindweed, buttercup, hemlock, nightshade, ragwort, St John's wort and speedwell.

No plants should be offered to your pet that are likely to have been sprayed with pesticide or treated with any other garden chemical. Collecting plants from the verges of roads can also pose a risk to your pet as lead contamination from exhaust fumes is likely.

**Titbits** Include a small amount of protein in the diet: this category covers a wide range of foods. However, they should be offered only in small quantities and should be considered as treats. Too much of any of these foods is likely to lead to digestive upsets.

Titbit foods include cheese, hamster hoops, mealworms, caterpillars, moths, earthworms, slices of hard boiled egg, slivers of red meat and flakes of cooked fish. Sweets, including chocolates, should not be included in the hamster's diet because they have a tendency to clog the cheek pouches, leading to infection. Commercially

*A solid firmly-based food bowl and a gravity-fed water bottle will help minimize the mess an energetic pet can make with its food and drink*

available hamster chocolate drops seem to be free from this problem.

# Drinking

**Water** Fresh water should always be available for the hamster to drink, either in a non-tip open bowl or preferably in a gravity-feed bottle, which avoids contamination of the water with food and faeces. Even though the hamster is a desert-living animal, this must not be taken as an excuse not to provide the hamster with water. Water is more readily available in the desert than is commonly believed, in the form of heavy morning dews and water stored in succulent plants.

Change your hamster's water supply daily, and clean and sterilize the bottle at least twice weekly. Check daily after each water change that the valve on the gravity-feed bottle is operating correctly, and check at least twice daily that the hamster has not piled up the litter until it touches the spout, as this will make the bottle leak.

**Milk** Hamsters enjoy small quantities of milk, especially pregnant and lactating females. Offer the milk in the evening, and remove it if not drunk within an hour. If the milk is left in the cage for too long it is likely to become soiled or turn sour, and in either case this could cause digestive upsets.

# Breeding

## Sexing hamsters

**Cubs** Until they are eight to ten days old, young female hamsters may be identified by their having two rows of seven nipples on the abdomen. Very soon afterwards the fur will have grown sufficiently dense for these to be totally concealed.

**Adults** The sexing of adults is relatively easy. The male has an elongated rear end, the female is more rounded. The genital openings in males are twice as far apart as those in the female. In adult males the testicles become very pronounced, forming a pair of bulges at the base of the tail.

*The difference in the sexes of adult hamsters is fairly conspicuous*

male                                    female

## Mating

Hamsters are prolific breeders capable of producing litters throughout the year, although there are fewer cubs in the litters during the winter. However, they are solitary by nature and should be kept in separate cages from six weeks of age to prevent possible fatal fighting as well as unwanted pregnancies.

# Breeding data

| | |
|---|---|
| Gestation period | 16 days (average) |
| Litter size | 2–8 (average) |
| Birth weight | $2\,g/\frac{1}{14}\,oz$ (average) |
| Eyes open | 5–7 days (approx.) |
| Weaning age | 21–27 days |
| Puberty | 45–60 days |
| Adult weight | $100\,g/3\frac{1}{2}\,oz$ (average) |
| Best age to breed | 12-plus weeks |
| Oestrus (or season) | every 4 days |
| Duration of oestrus | 4–23 hours (typically persists for an evening) |
| Retire from breeding | Males 15 months females 12 months |

Hamsters can breed for the first time at about eight weeks of age although it is usual to delay the first mating until at least the age of 12 weeks.

Males will mate at any time and females come into season every four days. The most obvious sign is a slight swelling and reddening of the vaginal opening. The female is introduced into the male's cage in the evening, this being the time when she is likely to be most receptive. (*Never* introduce the male into the female's cage as she will almost certainly attack him.)

If the female is ready to be mated, she will 'freeze' into an unmistakable posture. She will crouch forward with the head, body and hind limbs stretched out and with the tail raised. They will usually mate several times in quick succession, after which the female should be removed.

*When she is ready to mate a hamster will present her rear end to a male*

To be certain of a successful mating, the female must be put into the male's cage on four successive evenings. Some breeders recommend that they should be left together overnight but this leads to unnecessary fights and injuries. A period of 20 minutes together is probably a sufficient length of time.

## Pregnancy

The period of pregnancy varies from 15 to 18 days, most litters being produced 16 days after mating. This is the briefest gestation period of any mammal. By the middle of the second week after mating, the female will be showing obvious signs of pregnancy. During this week the bedding should be replaced and extra amounts supplied so that she can build a nest. The female will need additional protein and vitamins during the second half of pregnancy and while suckling the cubs. Fresh water must always be available with the bottle or bowl being topped up twice daily during the period the mother is suckling her young.

The nest should not be disturbed unnecessarily after the cubs have been born as this might endanger them. Litters vary in size from two to eight but litters of up to 16

*Baby hamsters are born naked and blind; their coats develop within a week and their eyes open in a few days*

have been known to be produced. When born, the cubs are about 3 cm (1 in) in length and are completely helpless, being born blind and hairless.

## Rearing the young

For the first week, the cubs will only consume their mother's milk. Their eyes open after five to seven days and a reasonable coat of hair has grown by the end of the week. By this time the cubs will start to eat solid food which has been hoarded by the mother, and will start eating finely chopped greens from about ten days of age.

They should be weaned by 25 days when the mother should be removed, and will each weigh about 25–40 g (1–1½ oz). Between four and six weeks the sexes should be separated to avoid mating.

The female can be mated again one month after giving birth, which is soon after the first litter has been weaned.

# Ailments

If your hamster is ill, seek veterinary advice as soon as possible. With many hamster diseases, by the time the symptoms have been recognized it is too late for successful treatment. The importance of hygiene in the handling of hamsters can not be overstressed (see Rules of Hygiene). Anyone suffering from a cold or influenza should not handle a hamster as the infection can be passed on to the animal.

## Rules of Hygiene

**1** Wash your hands after handling the hamster or cleaning out the cage.

**2** Wash the hamster's food dishes and water bottle separately from the household crockery.

**3** The hamster's food must be stored separately from the owner's food in sealable containers to prevent access by vermin.

**4** Animals must not be brought into or be allowed on to work surfaces within food preparation or food storage areas or kitchens.

**5** Never eat or drink while playing with a hamster or when cleaning out a cage.

**6** Young children must be supervised to ensure that these rules are kept.

## Ailments

**Cage paralysis** This distressing condition can be caused when there is little space available for exercise. Always provide plenty of exercise opportunities for the hamster such as an exercise wheel.

**Cannibalism** Female hamsters occasionally eat their cubs either because of disturbance or lack of milk. Piebald hamsters are likely to eat their young unless given absolute privacy after birth.

**Cheek pouches** Whole oats or barley in husks should be avoided in the food. The husks have sharp tips that can damage the lining of the pouches. Sticky foods such as

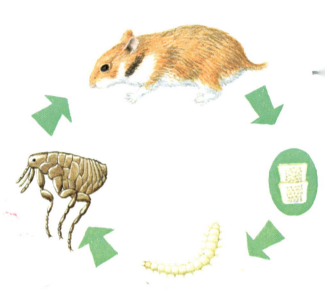

*Eggs laid by an internal parasite are expelled by the animal, hatch and develop, to be consumed by the host unless the chain is broken by dosing and thorough cleaning*

chocolate can become impacted in the pouches, and this leads to infection. The pouches must be washed out with water after being manually emptied by the hamster's owner.

**Common cold** Symptoms include sneezing and a sore and runny nose and eyes. The animals must be kept warm, the nose clear and they should be encouraged to eat. Change the bedding frequently. There may be a connection between colds and influenza in people and in the hamster handled by them. Stay away from your hamster if you have a cold, and also make sure the cage is not damp or in a draught.

**Constipation** Young hamsters about two weeks old may become constipated if they do not have access to water. They develop a swollen abdomen and distended anus. If their cage has a water bottle, make certain that the young can reach it. Feeding dampened green stuffs may help to prevent this condition.

**Lymphocytic choriomeningitis** This is a serious disease of hamsters that can be transmitted to humans. A hamster suffering from it will be very obviously ill, and must be taken to the vet. Hamsters bought from an accredited source will be free of this disease.

**Overgrown teeth** Hamsters are rodents and as such their teeth grow continually. Supply plenty of material for the hamster to gnaw. Check the teeth regularly; if they

*Like all rodents, hamsters have a pair of constantly growing incisor teeth at the centre front of their mouths separated from their cheek teeth by a small gap. Rodents wear their incisors down by continual gnawing, so hamsters should be provided with hard objects and food to prevent their teeth getting too long and needing a vet's attention*

become overgrown, take the hamster to the vet for them to be clipped short. Like humans, hamsters do not enjoy going to the dentist.

**Paralysis** As well as cage paralysis there are a number of similar ailments. Paralysis of the hind limbs affects males of certain strains aged between six and ten months of age. This may be an inherited condition. Falls and Vitamin E deficiency are other common causes. The hamster should be taken to the vet.

*Abcesses and infections can be gently squeezed and cleaned with a cloth or cotton wool moistened with diluted disinfectant*

**Salmonellosis** Affected hamsters lose weight and may develop diarrhoea. The infection can be spread to man and produce symptoms of food poisoning. Buy your hamster from accredited stock and wash your hands after handling or playing with your hamster.

**Skin diseases** In old age or in females recently weaned after large litters, patchy loss of hair and scaliness of the skin will occur. This is treated by improving the quality of the diet. Mange and ringworm can also cause hair loss but are usually associated with intense itching. These conditions can be transmitted to the owner.

**Tapeworms** Heavy infestations of tapeworms will cause diarrhoea which may contain mucus or blood. Live worms may be visible around the swollen and ulcerated anus. The affected animal will become lethargic and lose weight. Death can occur if the hamster does not receive veterinary treatment. Hamsters bought from an accredited source should be free of this disease.

**Wet tail** This disease is self-explanatory. Diarrhoea causes a wet tail and the droppings are soft and watery rather than being firm and dry. However, in 'wet tail' the symptoms are worse and there is also a discharge around the tail. The disease is extremely contagious for other hamsters, but it is found mainly in the wild. Stress and infection usually combine to cause this disease when it does occur in pets. Only prompt attention by a vet is likely to be successful.

**Broken bones and fractures** The most common cause is a fall or a fight. No home treatment is possible; seek veterinary assistance immediately.

# Exhibiting

Although a hamster bought from a pet shop is unlikely to be of a high enough quality to be a show winner, many shows do have classes where the novice exhibitor can gain experience. Hamsters are so popular that it is usually quite easy to find local shows with suitable classes. There are two main types of shows, the livestock section in agricultural and flower shows or fêtes, and those run under the auspices of the National Hamster Council (NHC).

In agricultural shows, small mammals such as rabbits, guinea pigs, gerbils and hamsters are usually included in the pet show which is just one part of the livestock section, which will also include poultry, ducks, goats and other farm animals. There is a tendency for a single judge to cover all the small mammals and the standard of judging may not be as high as in the NHC shows.

The NHC was formed in the 1950s and is the coordinating body for the three regional clubs:

**Yorkshire** This club covers the North-west of England; the North-east of England and Scotland.

**Midlands** This club covers the West Midlands, East Midlands and Wales.

**South** This club covers the remainder of England including the West country, London and the home counties.

The membership fee also buys you a monthly magazine, *The National Hamster Council Journal*, in which a show diary is published. The NHC is the governing body controlling the clubs and it lays down the show rules and the show standards. The serious exhibitor will be showing at events run by the NHC. Visit these shows to look at the winning hamsters and to watch the judging as important preliminaries to your show career. It is from the people exhibiting at these shows that you could try to buy the quality stock from which to develop your own strain of show hamster.

The first and most important prerequisite of a show hamster is that the animal should be tame and used to being handled. Taming can start just before the cubs are weaned, when they emerge from the nest to take their first solid food (earlier attempts to touch the cubs may provoke the mother into attacking you). Any hamster showing aggression towards the judges will be marked down in the final assessment.

Successful showing depends on two separate skills, the preparation and the presentation of the hamster.

## Preparation

For several days before the show the hamster should only be offered dry food. This avoids any potential problems caused by feeding fruit and vegetables: these include diarrhoea, which may soil the coat, as may the juice from the greenstuffs.

**Grooming** This should intensify leading up to the show, especially with the long-haired varieties; you can use a cat grooming brush or a tooth brush or, as many exhibitors prefer, a grooming box. This is a well ventilated box such as a 5 litre (2 gal) ice cream container, well filled with fresh, soft hay and whitewood sawdust, into which the hamster will burrow, thus grooming itself.

*A toothbrush makes an inexpensive grooming item for a hamster's coat*

Two hours in the grooming box is perfectly long enough – there is little extra benefit in leaving the hamster in there any longer. Complete the grooming with a little gentle brushing, and you can apply a final shine to the coat with a silk handkerchief.

**Removing stains** You can clean stains out of the fur by dampening the affected area and gently rubbing in cornflour: allow this to dry and then gently brush the cornflour out. You can repeat the process if the stain proves stubborn. When wetting the fur, ensure that the hamster is kept in a warm environment to avoid any problems such as chills.

However, before using this technique of stain removal, do check with the show organizers or your local club to see if it is permitted – in some, it is not.

On the day of the show, transfer the hamster to a special carrying box and, if the show is some distance away, provide it with something to eat on the way: dried food and a slice of raw potato (for moisture) should be enough.

# Presentation

At the show, transfer your hamster to a special show cage, measuring 15 cm (6 in) high on a base 20 × 15 cm (8 × 6 in). There is no bedding in the cage, nor should food be provided during judging. The show cage should contain only white sawdust as a flooring.

As the animals will be judged in these cages it is important that they have a uniform appearance and plans for making your own cages are available from the NHC, although second-hand cages are often available at club meetings.

During judging the only identification on the cage will be a small coded label stuck on the top left-hand corner of the cage. These precautions should ensure that no bias enters the judge's decision.

**Standards** The NHC standards state that a judge should be looking for 'a hamster of good size with a broad, rounded skull and a short blunt un-ratlike face. Ears should be large, set well apart and upstanding when the hamster is awake. The fur should be soft, short and dense, except in the case of long-haired hamsters. In the long-haired variety the hair should be long, soft and fine in texture'.

Points are awarded in the following categories: colour and markings, type, fur, size, condition, eyes and ears. The perfect hamster will gain 100 points, allocated as follows:

| | |
|---|---|
| Colour and markings | 30 |
| Type | 15 |
| Fur | 15 |
| Size | 15 |
| Condition | 15 |
| Eyes | 5 |
| Ears | 5 |

Hamsters will be disqualified if they are aggressive or obviously ill, or if food or bedding are present in the cage, or if the show cage carries markings which may identify the exhibitor. Other defects such as obesity can cost up to five penalty points.

*As well as being a delightful pet, a hamster can win awards and prizes for a proud owner*

# Useful addresses

National Hamster Council, Mrs J. Newall, 4 Beech Mere Rise, Etching Hill, Rugely, Staffordshire.

The Royal Society for the Prevention of Cruelty to Animals, Causeway, Horsham, East Sussex RH12 1HG.

Small Animals Genetic Circle, 179 Pavilion Road, Worthing, East Sussex

# Index

**Photographic acknowledgments**
Animal Photography 22, 43; Bruce Coleman – Jane
Burton 9, 18, 19, Hans Reinhard 16; Nature
Photographers – Michael Leach 28; The Photo Source
– Colour Library International 23; Spectrum Colour
Library 20, 36–37

Illustrations by Linden Artists (John Rignall)